brain-science

COLORING FOR AGILITY AND FAST LEARNING

DR STAN RODSKI B.Ec., D.Sc(BIO)
PEAK PERFORMANCE NEUROSCIENTIST

hardie grant books

About the Authors

Dr Stan Rodski
Neuroscientist

Stan has worked as a psychologist for over 30 years. Currently, he is involved in neuroscientific research around the issues of stress and how best to deal with it in our personal, family and work life.

He first qualified as a registered psychologist in 1985 and completed his doctorate in Bio Science in 1994.

Stan has worked in private practice in Australia and internationally, working with individuals, elite sporting teams and many Australian and international Top 500 companies.

Most recently he has been applying brain science research to areas such as improved sleep, fatigue and stress, and energy revitalization and management.

This research has led to a number of programs that he facilitates all over the world. The coloring book series was initially available through these programs where its success in creating a calming effect was first recognized and established.

Jack Dowling
Jack is an architecture student at RMIT University in Melbourne, Australia; co-director of online art community, Artselect; and illustrator for the adult coloring series of books. Jack describes finding patterns as a creative and iterative process. He hopes readers will similarly apply their own creative intuition, allowing the mind to relax and enjoy the meditative qualities that come from these exercises.

CONTENTS

Introduction

Welcome to *Brain*-science, a coloring book for adults based on neuroscience.

In our first book, *Anti*-stress, we focused on

- how the brain calms from pressured beta waves to calm alpha waves during the process of coloring

- how the brain can be further calmed by the use of certain colors; and finally

- how we can use the principles of brain neuroplasticity (brain rewiring) to use all of our brain to relax.

As children, we used coloring to develop our muscle strength and stamina for the muscles we use to write with. It also allowed us to develop hand-eye control, attention and focus to stay in what we call 'spatial lines'. The object was to stay within the lines to develop our fine motor skills.

As adults, coloring presents us with new opportunities. When we color, it has a calming effect for most of us and can be an excellent step to achieving a far greater state of relaxation.

In elderly people, it can also be used for the same objective as when we were children: as a skillful activity to strengthen our fine motor coordination and skills.

In this book we look at

- the brain's 'fight or flight' response and the effect of relaxation

- how repetition, pattern and focus are used in our drawings to further relax and energize the brain; and finally

- helping our brain to be more agile and a 'fast learner'.

Enjoy and relax as you immerse yourself in the patterns created by my co-contributor and graphic artist, Jack Dowling.

Dr Stan Rodski – Neuroscientist

PART ONE

Fight or flight

HERE, WE EXPLORE THE BRAIN'S 'FIGHT OR FLIGHT' RESPONSE AND ITS EFFECT ON RELAXATION. HUMANS ARE VERY VISUAL CREATURES: MUCH OF WHAT WE DO, THINK AND REACT TO IS DONE ON A VISUAL BASIS.

WHEN WE FEEL PRESSURED AND STRESSED OUR BRAIN REACTS IN WHAT IS OFTEN CALLED THE 'FIGHT OR FLIGHT' RESPONSE

LET'S LOOK AT THIS A LITTLE MORE CLOSELY.

FIGHT OR FLIGHT RESPONSE

- Reacts 'instantly' (in milliseconds)

- Visual cortex sees the danger and works directly with the deep limbic system that sends messages to the muscles to move

- 'Knee jerk' reactions

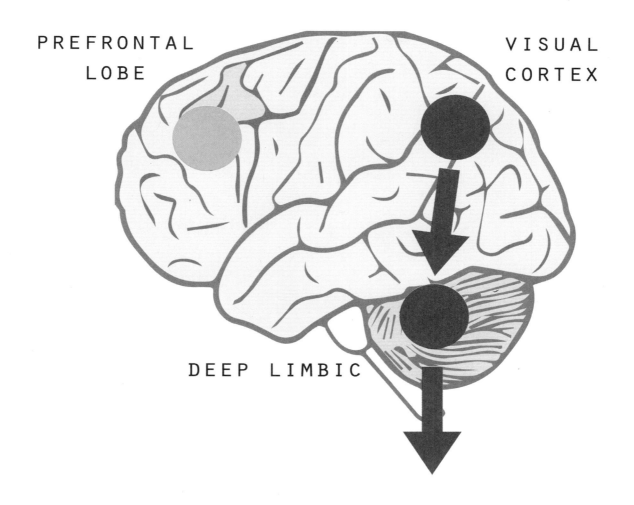

PREFRONTAL LOBE

VISUAL CORTEX

DEEP LIMBIC

NORMAL MODE

- Reacts 'slowly' (in a second)

- Visual inputs sent to the pre frontal cortex 'command centre' for processing before actions sent to the deep limbic and onwards to the body

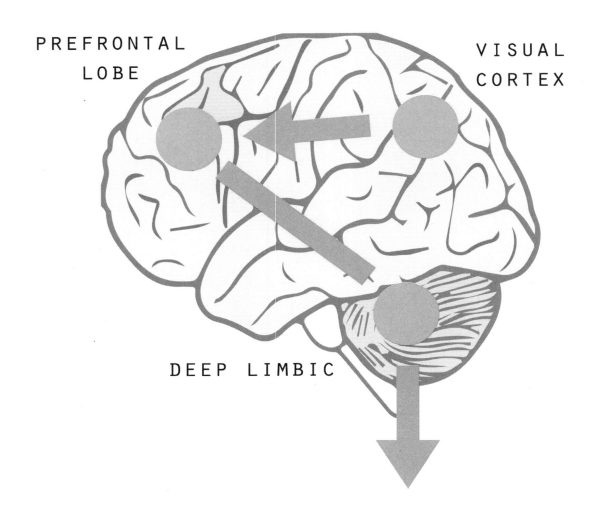

PREFRONTAL
LOBE

VISUAL
CORTEX

DEEP LIMBIC

WHAT WE NEED TO DO

TO MOVE FROM 'FIGHT OR FLIGHT' MODE TO 'NORMAL MODE', WE NEED TO BE CALM — THE CALM THAT IS PRODUCED BY COLORING.

COLORING THAT IS PATTERNED, REPETITIOUS AND FOCUSED HELPS THE BRAIN TO LEARN TO RELAX AND BECOME MORE MINDFUL.

TIME
TO RELAX

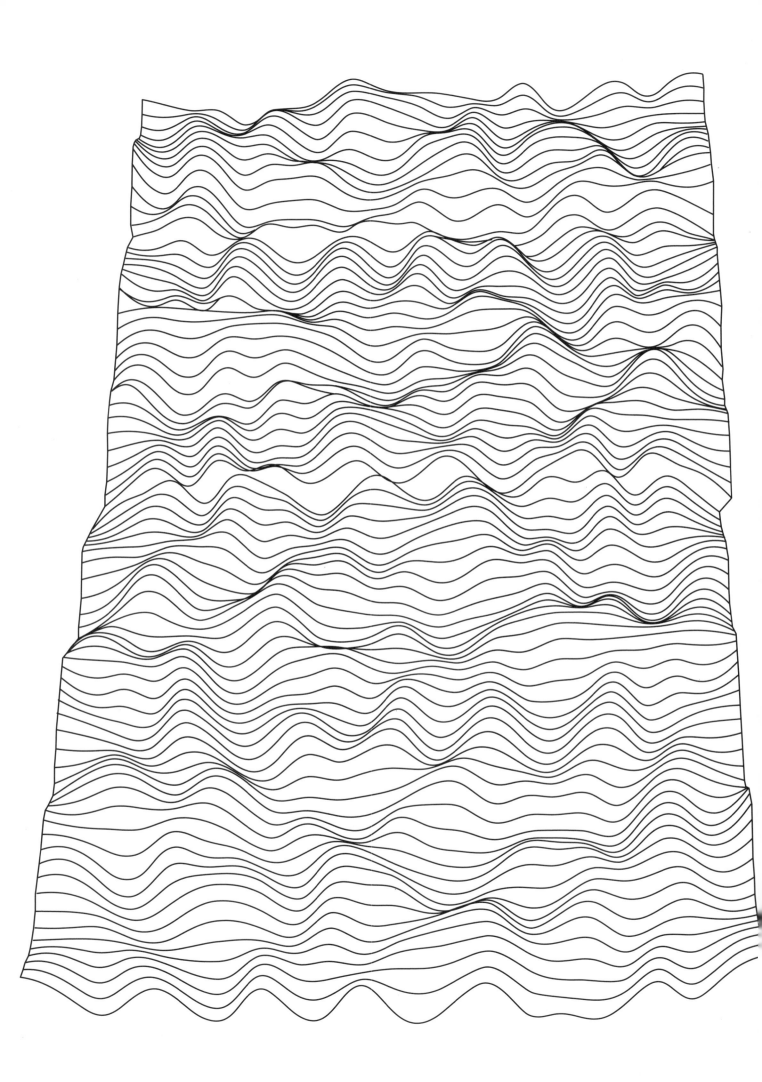

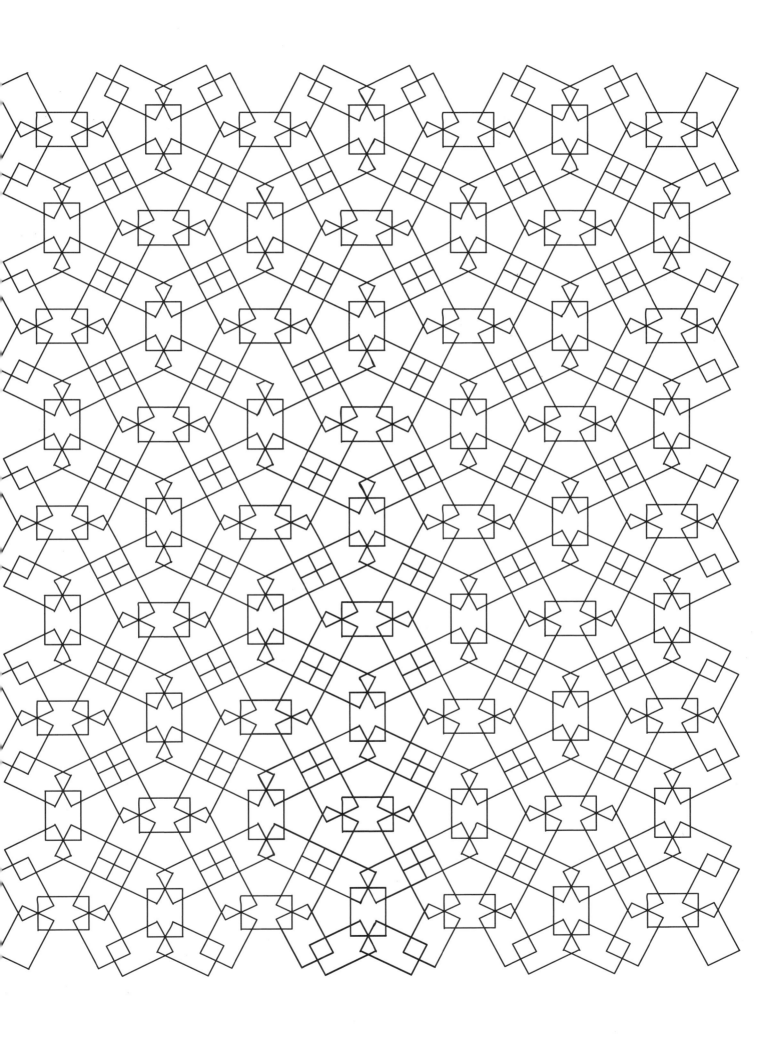

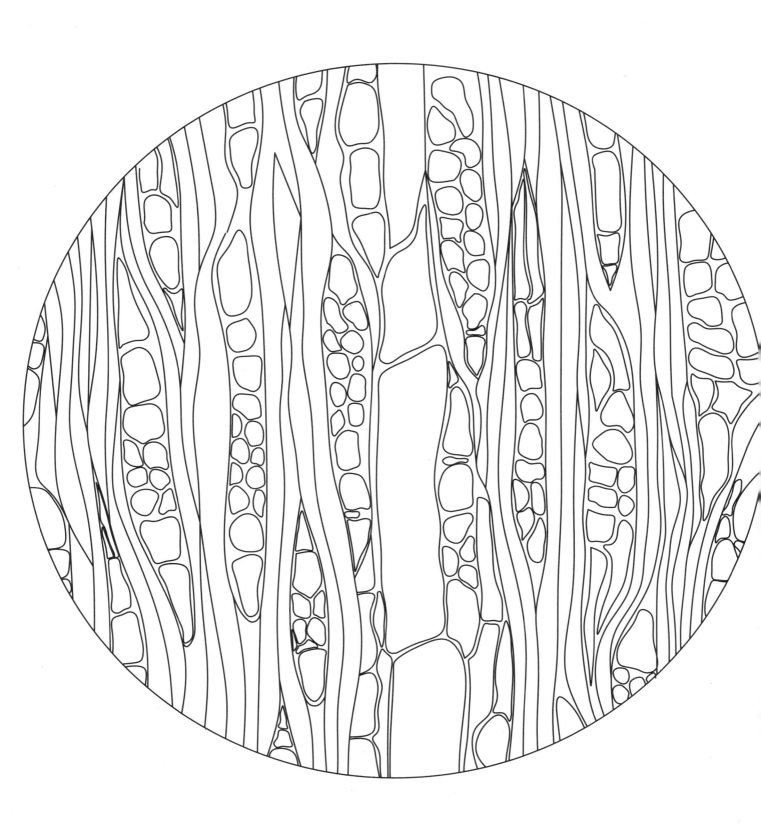

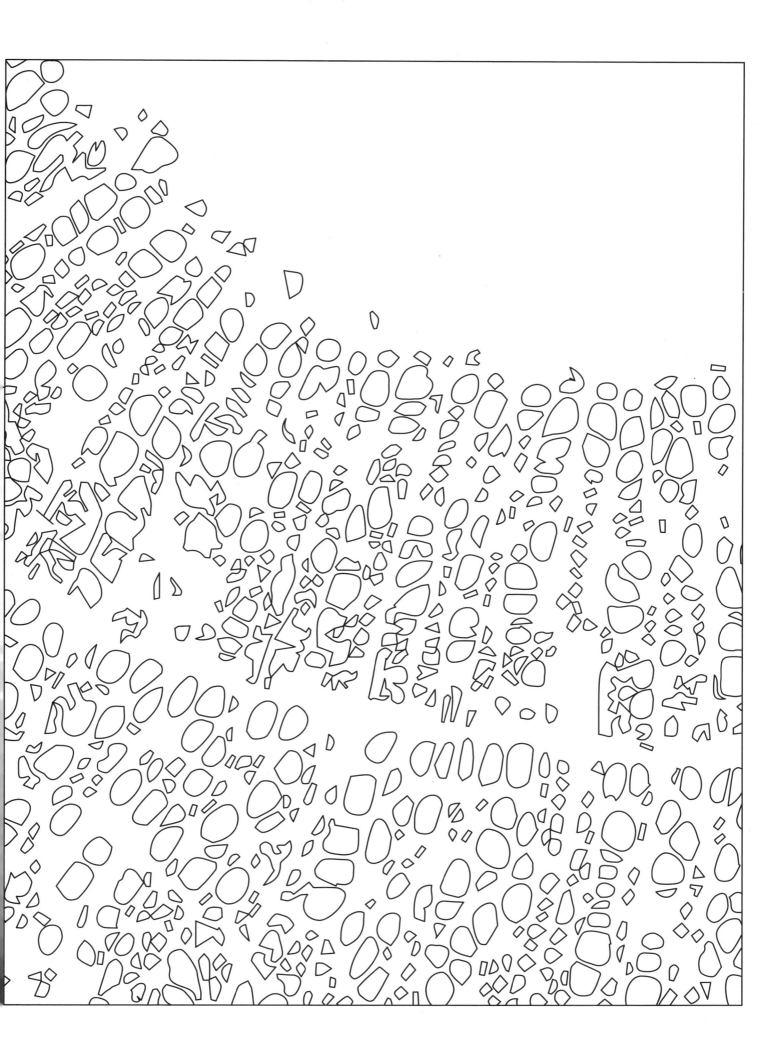

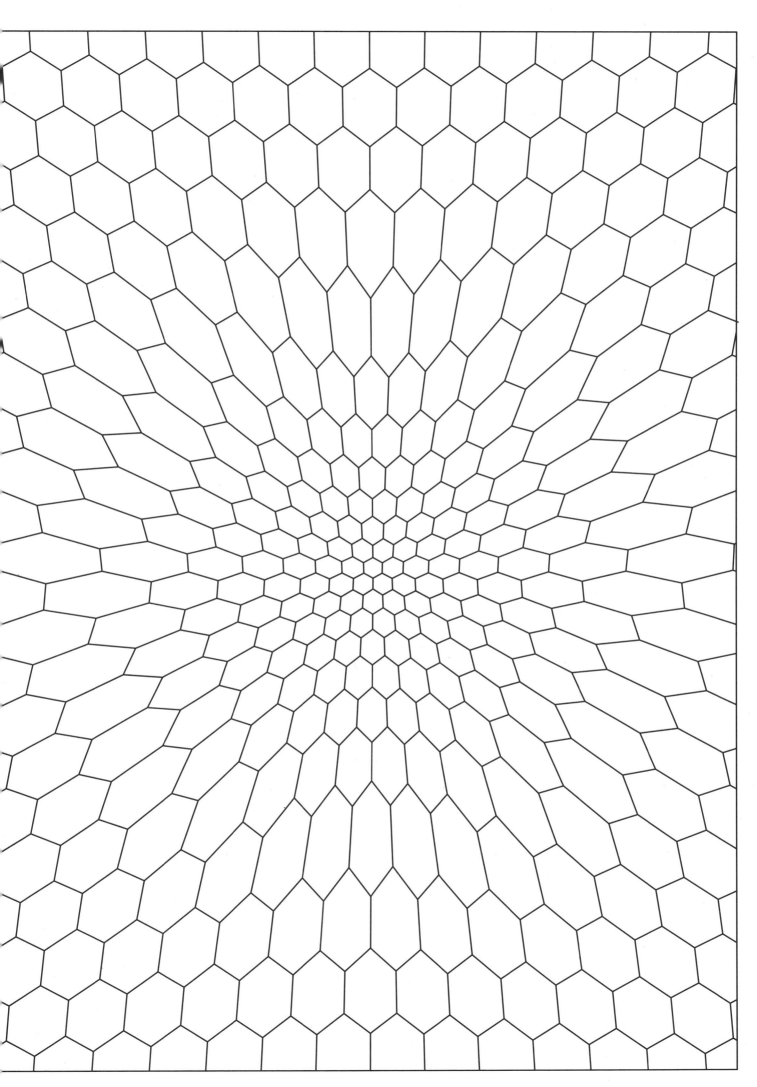

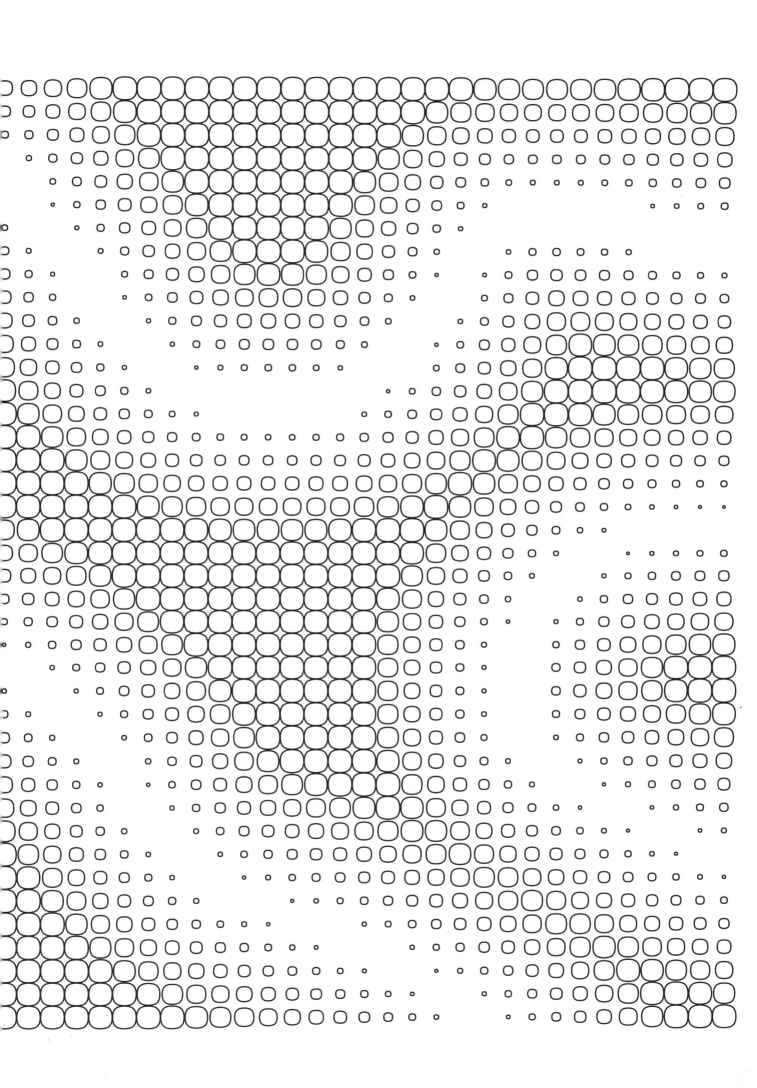

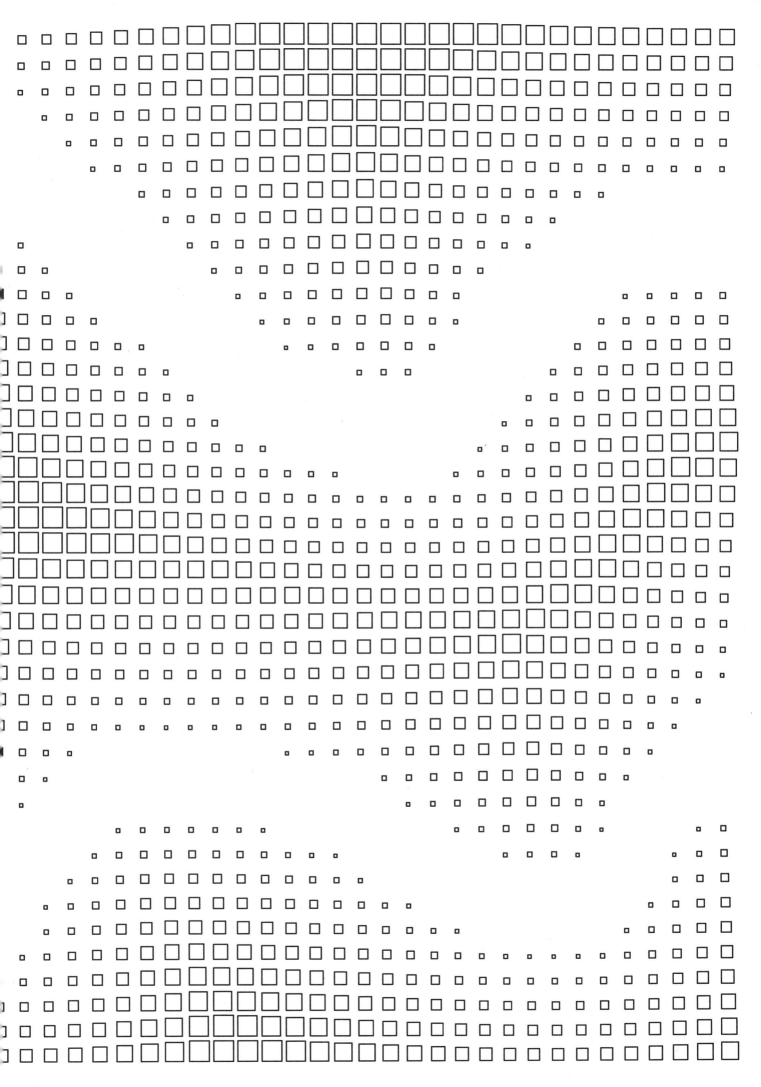

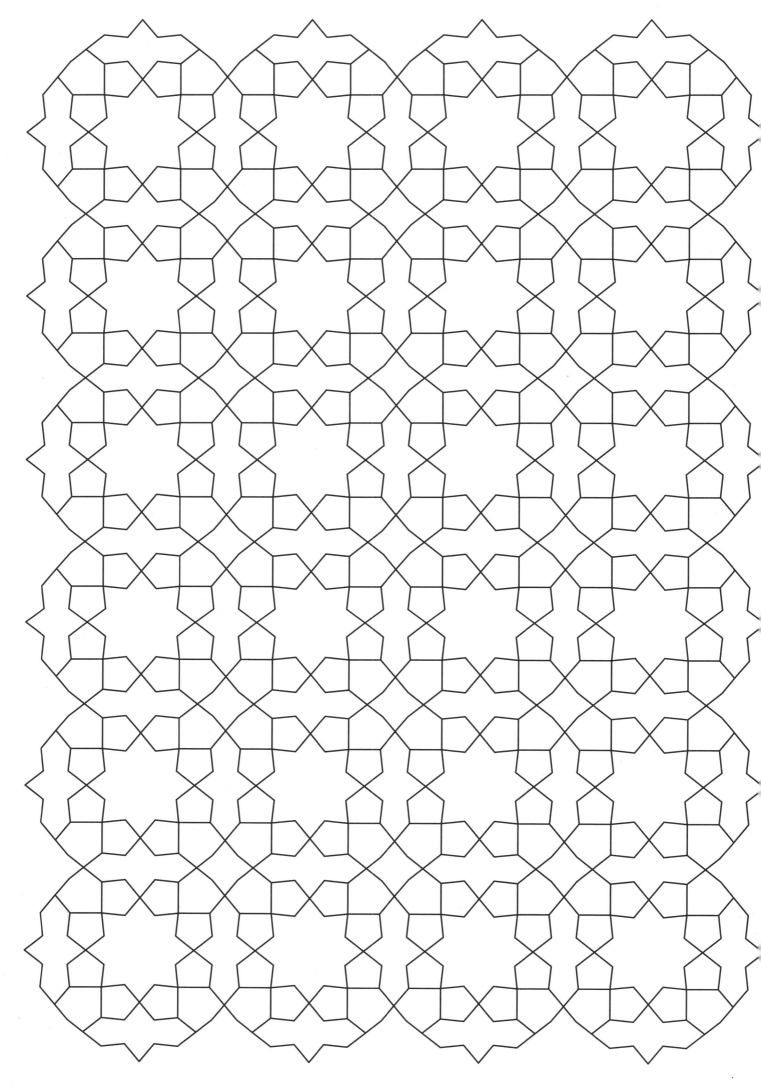

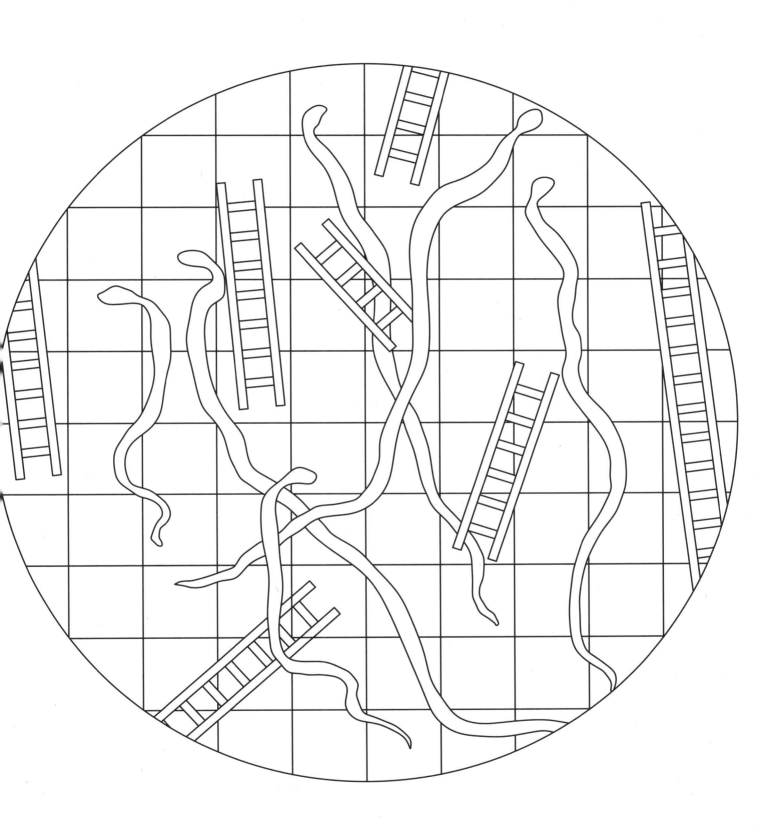

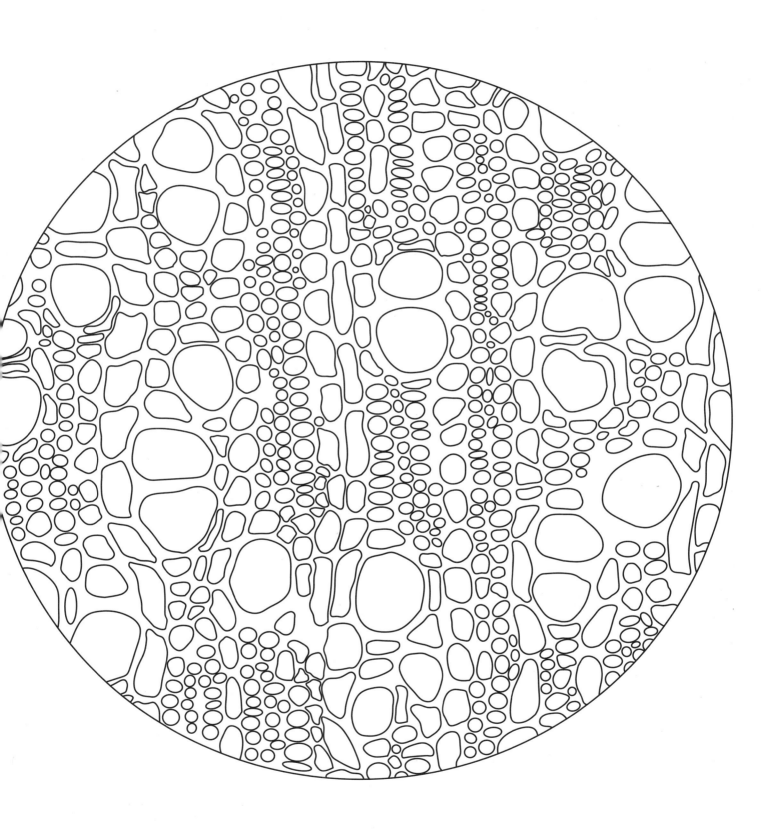

PART TWO
Repetition, pattern, focus

HERE WE EXPLORE HOW REPETITION, PATTERN AND FOCUS ARE USED IN OUR DRAWINGS TO FURTHER RELAX THE BRAIN AND HELP IT ENERGIZE.

OFTEN OUR BRAIN HAS LEARNT PATTERNS AND RESPONSES TO THINGS THAT HAVE HAPPENED IN OUR LIVES. THESE BIG, AND SOMETIMES NOT SO BIG, EVENTS HAVE BEEN REINFORCED SIMPLY THROUGH REPETITION.

WITH OUR BETTER UNDERSTANDING OF BRAIN SCIENCE, WE NOW KNOW IT IS POSSIBLE TO CHANGE OUR REACTIONS TO STRESS.

THE KEY IS TO CONTINUOUSLY CREATE NEW PATHWAYS AND CONNECTIONS TO BREAK AWAY STUCK NEURAL PATTERNS IN THE BRAIN.

WHAT WE NEED TO DO IS FOCUS

BUT TO STAY FOCUSED WE NEED TO BE CALM. THE CALM THAT IS PRODUCED BY COLORING.

COLORING THAT IS PATTERNED, REPETITIOUS AND FOCUSED HELPS THE BRAIN TO LEARN TO RELAX.

BY THE TIME WE HAVE REACHED THE AGE OF 25 WE HAVE SO MANY EXISTING PATHWAYS (REACTIONS) OUR BRAIN RELIES ON THAT IT IS VERY HARD TO FREE THEM. BUT THE MORE RELAXED WE ARE, THE BETTER OUR BRAIN PERFORMS.

WITHOUT THE RIGHT ENVIRONMENT TO ENABLE CHANGE, OUR BRAIN WON'T BE ABLE TO FOCUS ON WHAT'S NEEDED TO CREATE NEW NEURONS. YOU WILL BE STUCK IN SURVIVAL MODE, STAYING ON WELL-DEFINED PATHS WHICH MINIMIZE RISK.

OUR BRAIN NEEDS A MASSIVE AMOUNT OF HYDRATION (WATER), NUTRIENTS (BLOOD SUPPLY) AND REST (CALM) TO ENERGIZE ITSELF.

WHILE WE ARE COLORING, WE ARE BUILDING-UP ENERGY TO KEEP OUR BRAIN FLEXIBLE AND 'PLASTIC'. THIS ALLOWS THE BRAIN TO LEARN, UNLEARN AND RELEARN.

THE DRAWINGS YOU ARE COLORING REINFORCE THE BRAIN'S DESIRE FOR REPETITION, PATTERN AND FOCUS WHEN IT IS STRESSED OR PREPARING FOR STRESS.

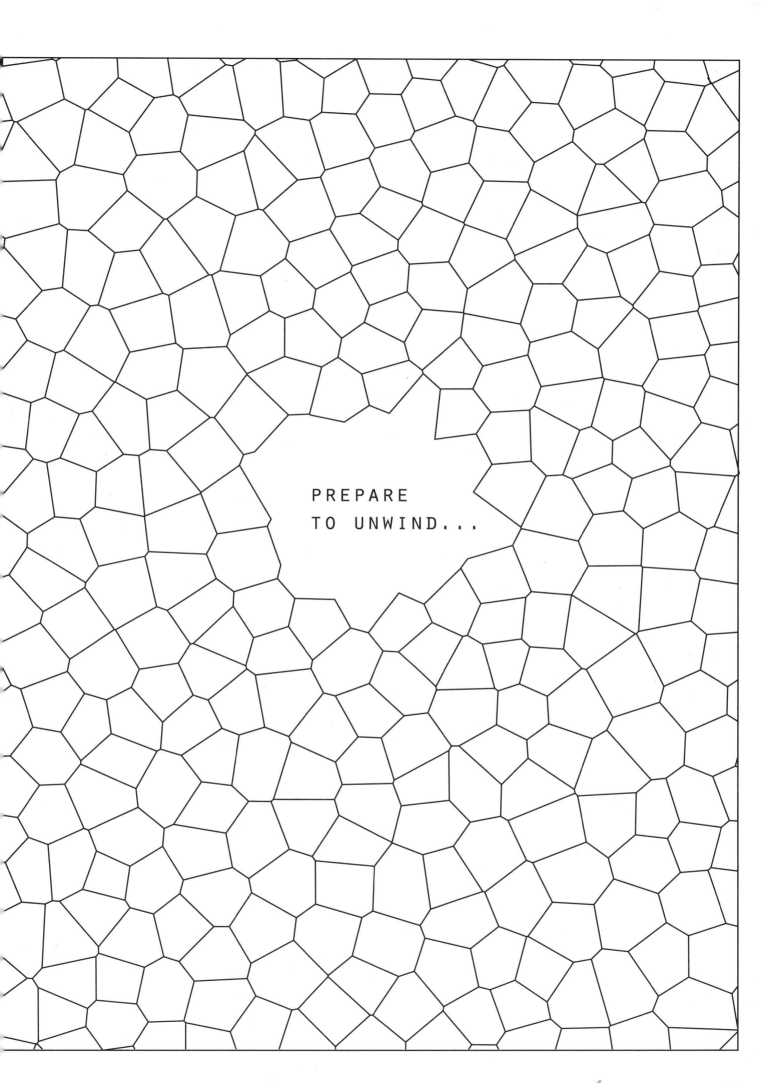

PREPARE
TO UNWIND...

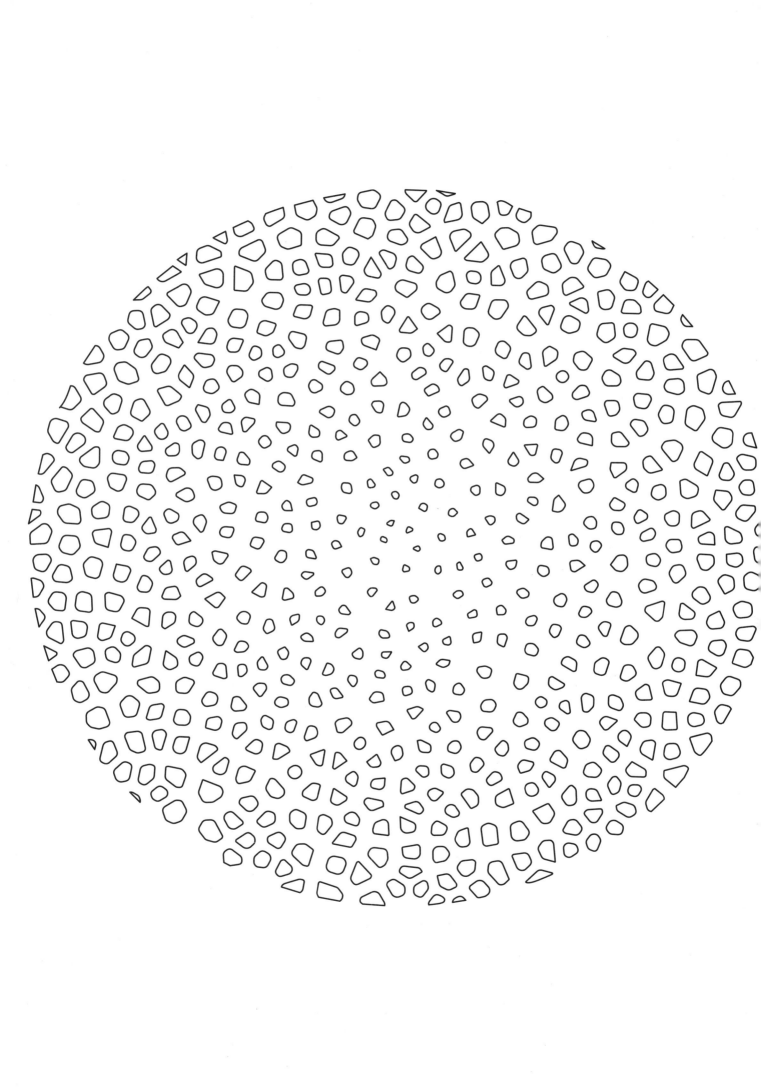

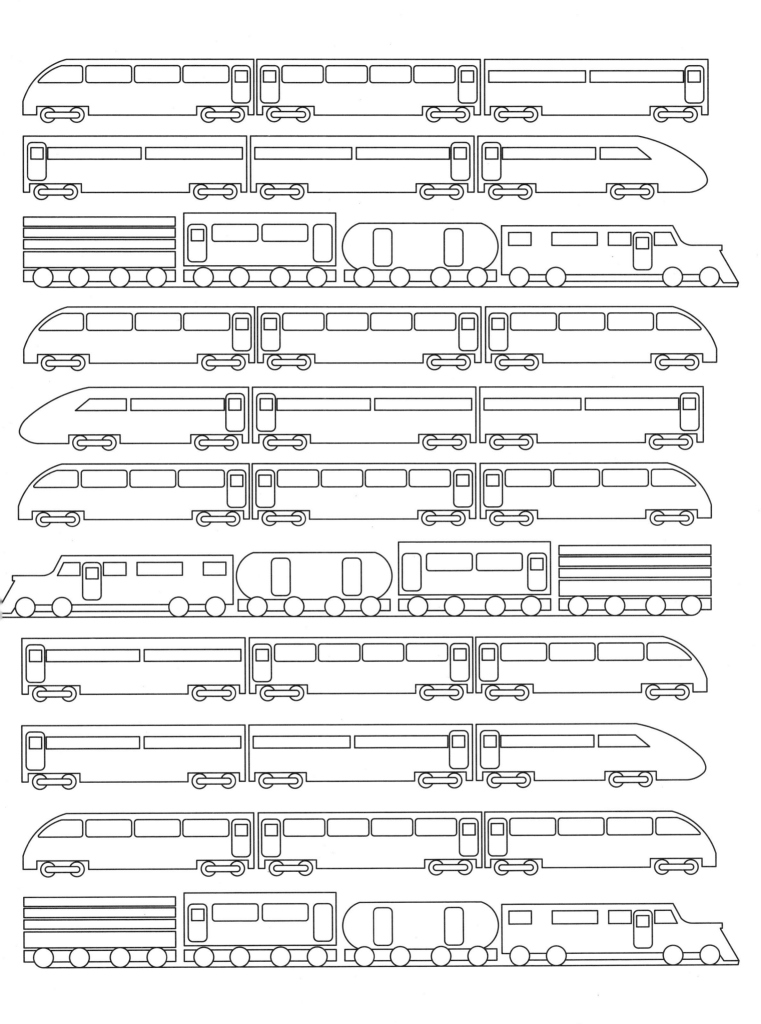

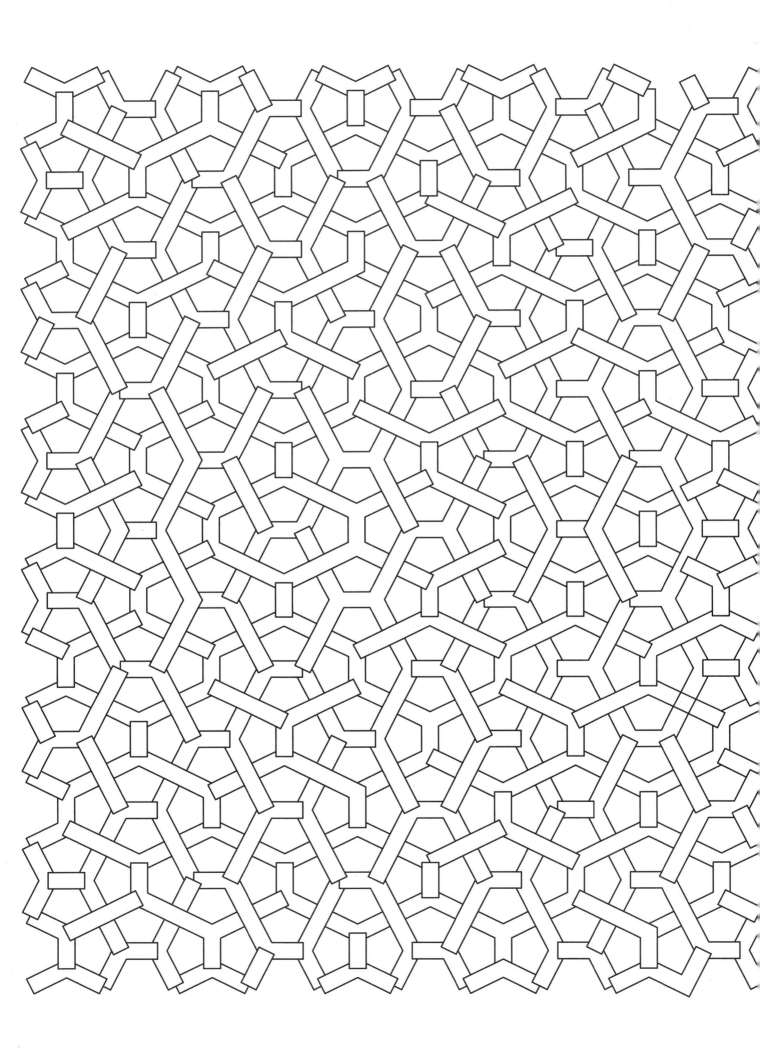

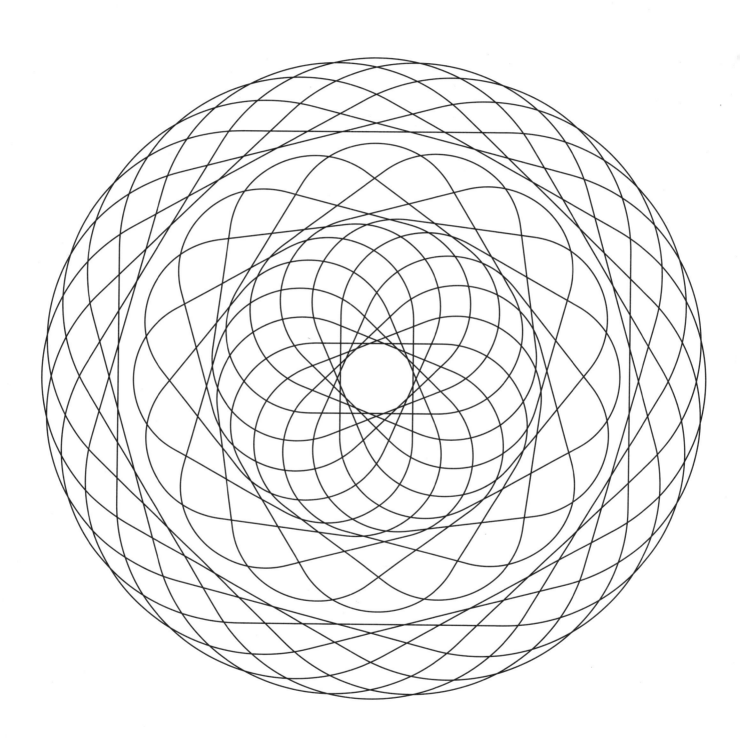

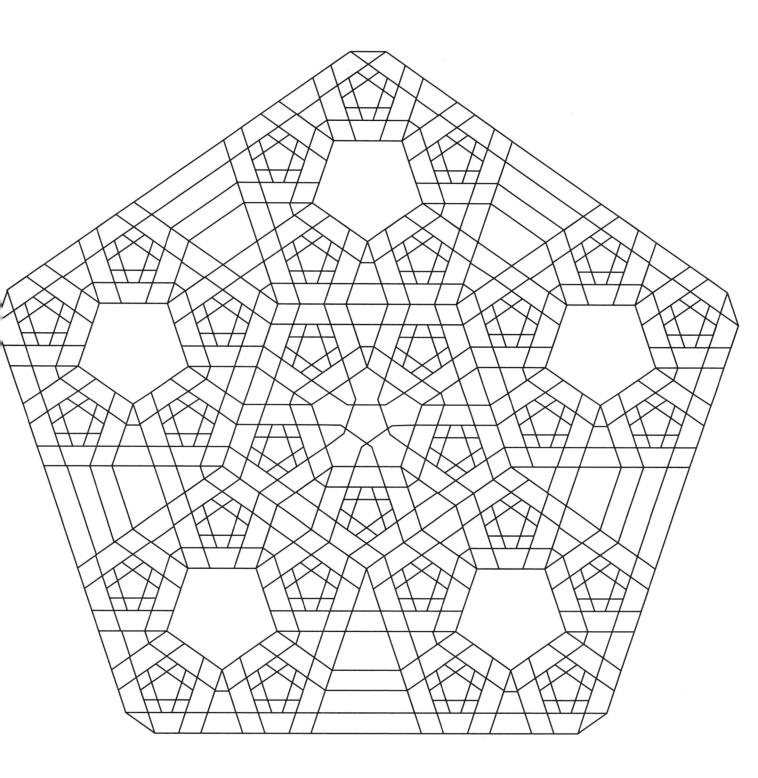

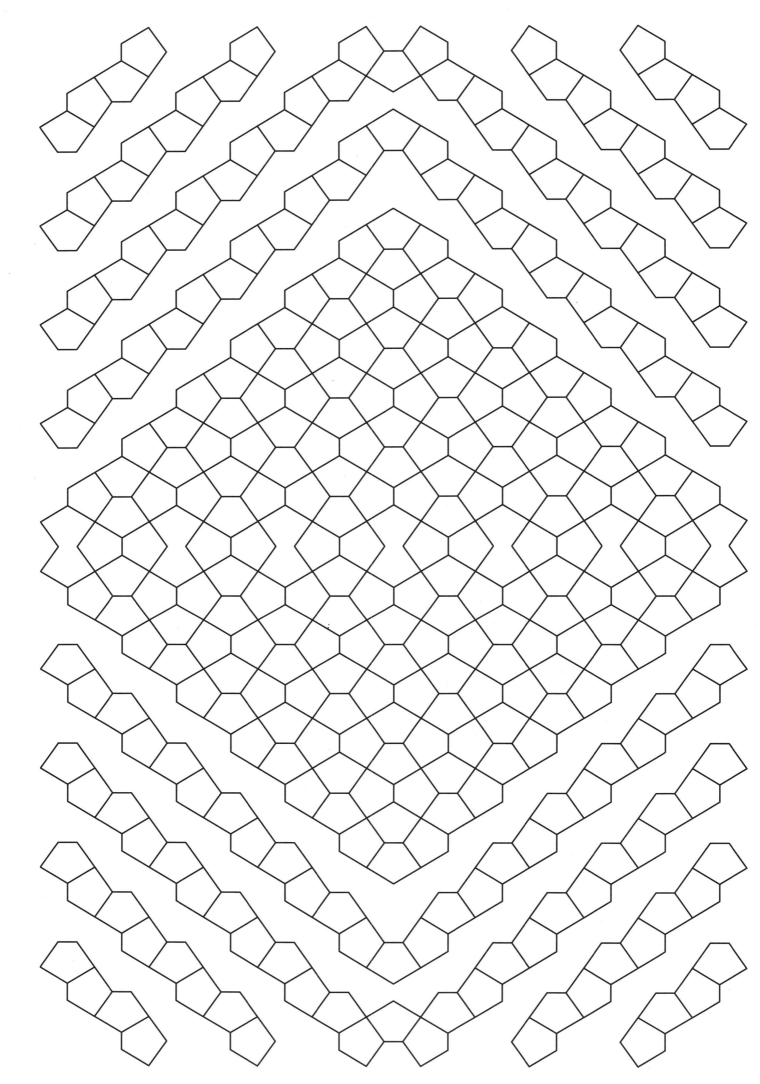

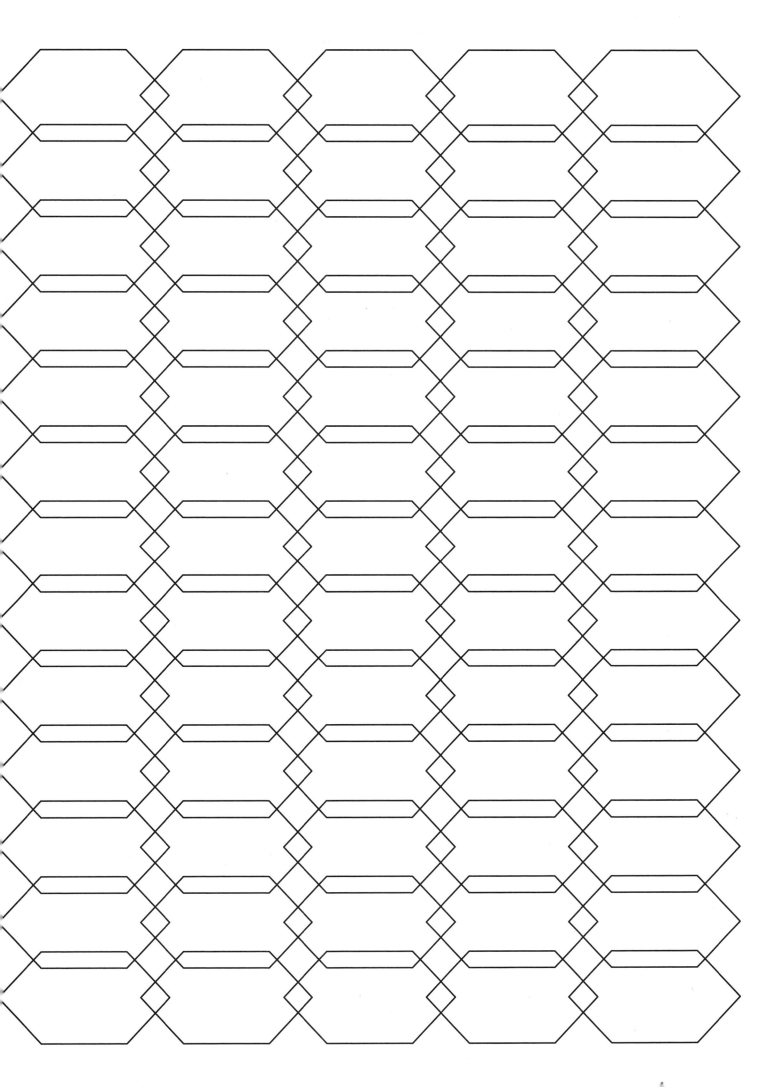

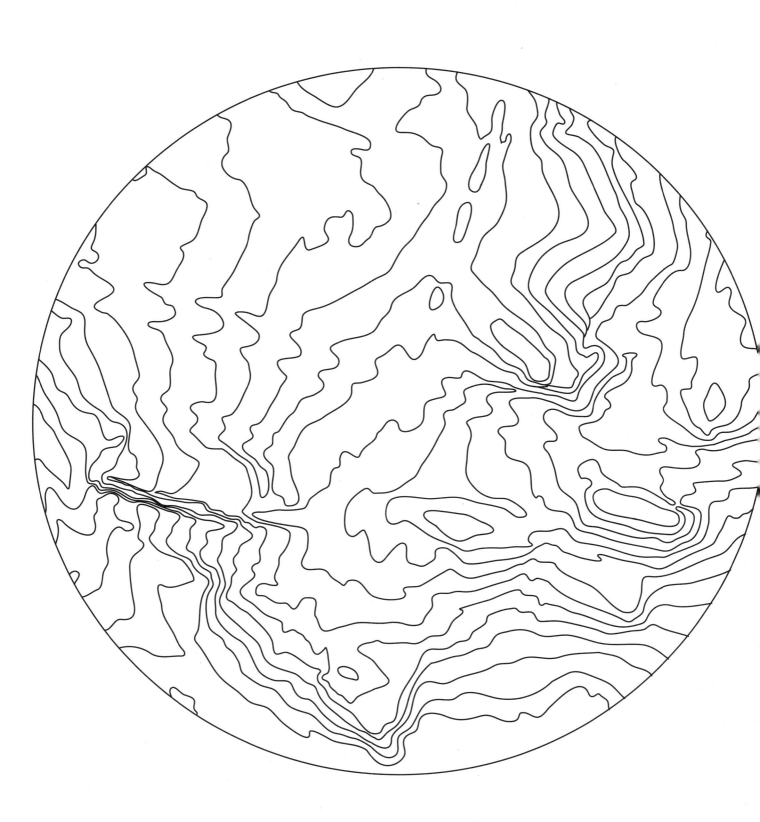

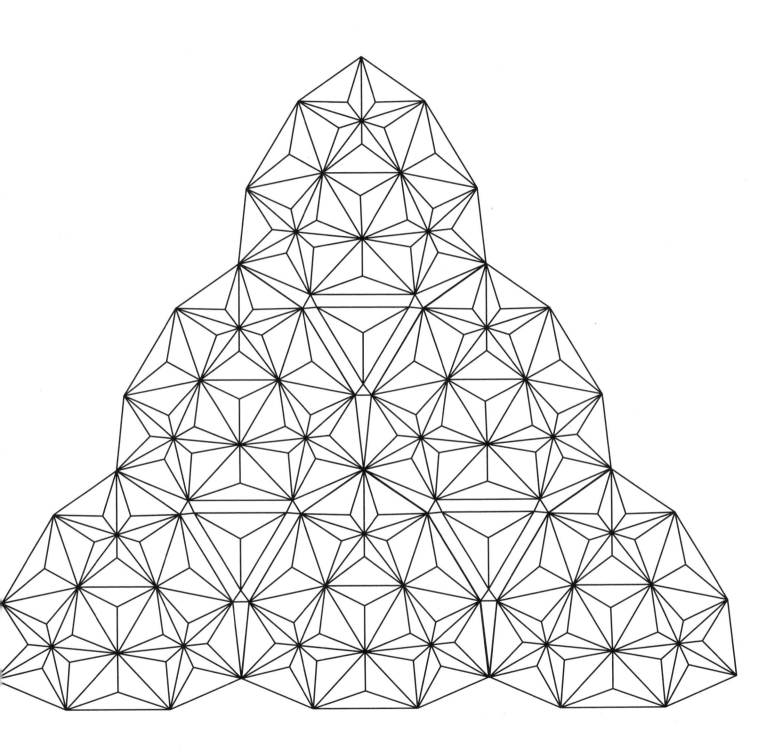

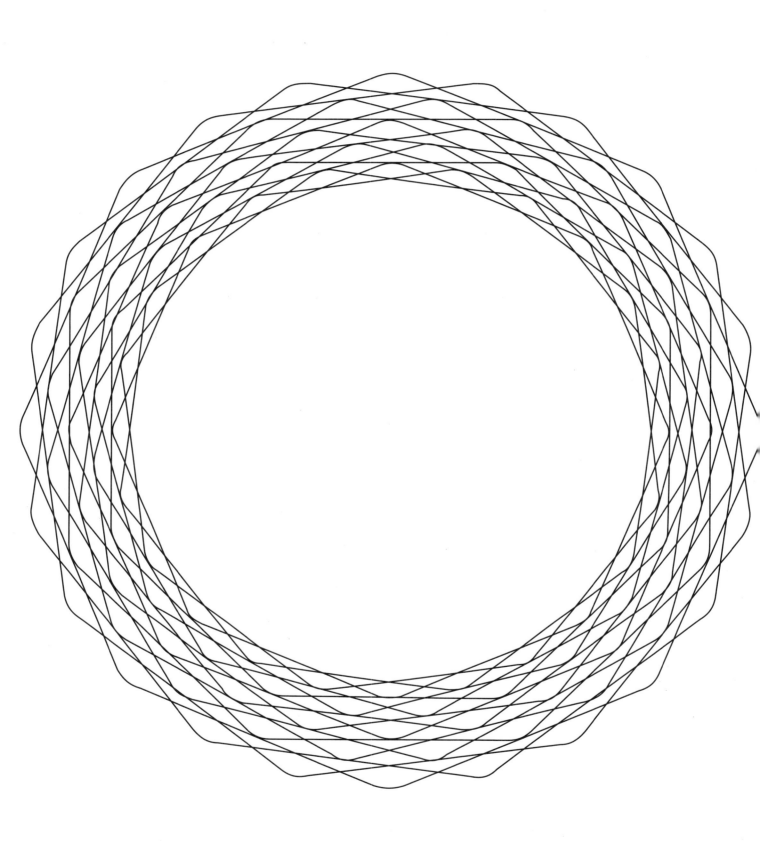

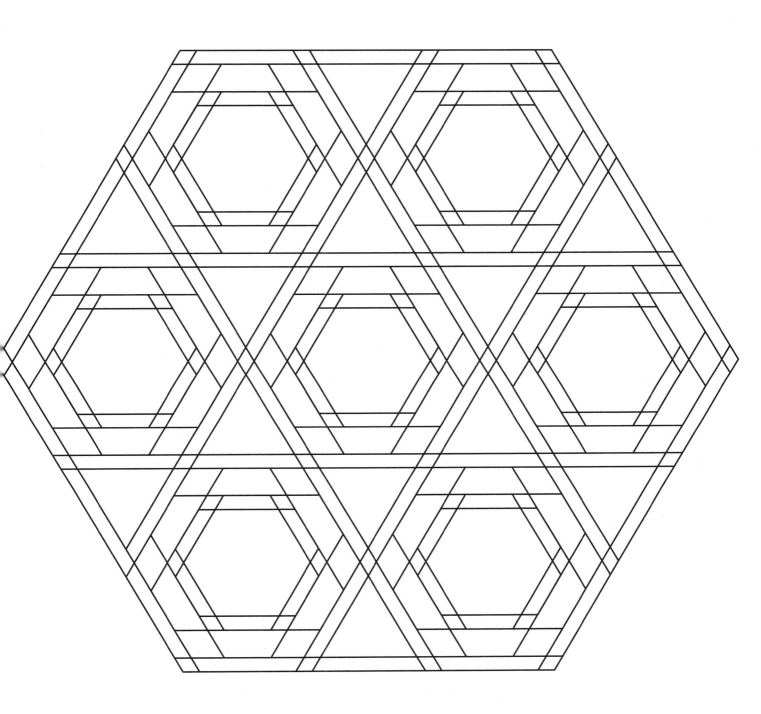

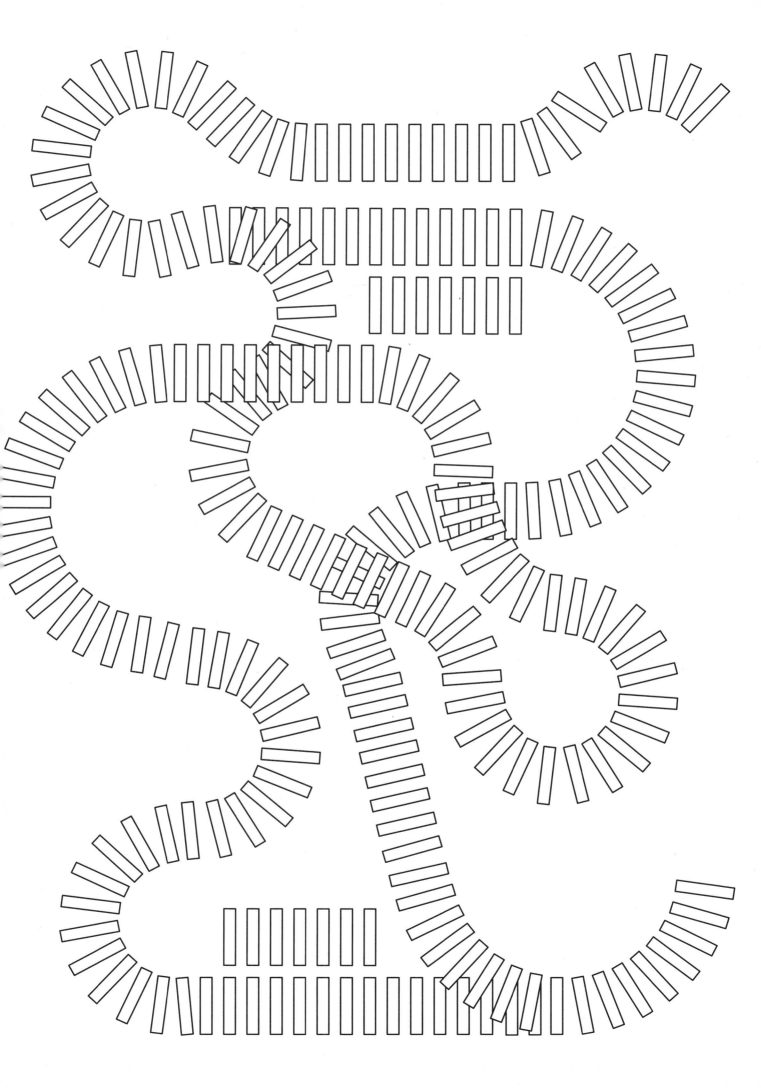

PART THREE

Agility and fast learning

IN THIS THIRD PART WE EXPLORE HELPING OUR BRAIN TO BE A MORE AGILE AND FAST LEARNER. FOR THOSE OF US WHO WANT OUR BRAIN TO BE MORE AGILE, WE HAVE TO FOCUS ON PARTS OF THE BRAIN THAT WE USE LESS FREQUENTLY.

THE NEW TASK HAS TO BE SO CHALLENGING THAT WE FEEL MENTALLY AND PHYSICALLY EXHAUSTED AFTER PRACTICING IT. THIS MEANS WE ARE FORCING OUR BRAIN TO WORK IN WAYS IT IS UNACCUSTOMED TO.

THIS IS THE ONLY WAY WE ACTUALLY GROW NEW NEURONS STRONG ENOUGH TO CONNECT WITH EXISTING NEURONS AND CAN FORM NEW PATHWAYS.

COLORING PROVIDES AN EXCELLENT PREPARATION FOR OUR BRAIN TO ENTER INTO SUCH DEMANDING TASKS.

YOU MAY WANT TO LEARN A NEW LANGUAGE OR PLAY A MUSICAL INSTRUMENT (OR A DIFFERENT ONE) AND THIS WILL STIMULATE YOUR BRAIN THROUGH THE ENERGY INTENSIVENESS OF THE CHALLENGE.

MANY CHALLENGES WE TAKE ON REQUIRE THIS ENERGY INTENSIVENESS. CHALLENGES SUCH AS COMPLEX PROBLEM SOLVING, MEMORIZING COMPLEX CONCEPTS, PLANNING, STRATEGIZING, SELF REFLECTION, REGULATING OUR EMOTIONS, SELF CONTROL AND WILLPOWER ALL NEED ENERGY PROVIDED BY THE BRAIN.

BRAIN AGILITY IS ENHANCED AND OPTIMIZED IF WE COME AT THESE CHALLENGES FROM A CALM AND STRESS-FREE STATE THAT CAN BE CREATED THROUGH THE ACT OF COLORING.

YOU CAN'T JUST LEARN A NEW LANGUAGE OR PLAY A NEW INSTRUMENT AND NEVER THINK ABOUT IT AGAIN — YOU'LL FORGET WHAT YOU HAVE LEARNED.

NEW CONNECTIONS AND PATHWAYS ARE FRAGILE.

THROUGH REPETITION AND PRACTICE FROM A CALM STATE (USING COLORING), THESE CONNECTIONS CAN BE FIRMLY ESTABLISHED AND BECOME HABITUAL OR DEFAULT (AUTOMATIC) BEHAVIORS. WHEN YOU HAVE PRACTICED (AN INSTRUMENT OR LANGUAGE) FOR 20 MINUTES, RELAX WITH COLORING FOR 10 MINUTES BEFORE PRACTICING AGAIN FOR 20 MINUTES — WATCH WHAT HAPPENS TO YOUR LEARNING AGILITY.

THIS TECHNIQUE PROVIDES AN EXCELLENT ALTERNATIVE FOR BUSY PEOPLE WHO NEED A WAY TO RELAX, MEDITATE AND PRACTICE MINDFULNESS EASILY.

OUR AIM: TO PAY ATTENTION TO SOMETHING (IN THIS CASE COLORING) IN A PARTICULAR WAY, ON PURPOSE, IN THE PRESENT MOMENT, NON-JUDGEMENTALLY.

STEPS:

1: SET YOUR INTENTION TO USE YOUR COLORING BOOK AT LEAST ONCE A DAY FOR 15 MINUTES.

2: CULTIVATE AWARENESS. DURING COLORING, PAY ATTENTION TO WHAT IS HAPPENING IN THE MOMENT AND ACKNOWLEDGE AND DISMISS DISTRACTIONS.

3: REGULATE YOUR ATTENTION. BE AWARE WITHOUT CHANGING WHAT YOU ARE DOING. REFOCUS YOUR ATTENTION DURING COLORING IF OTHER THOUGHTS APPEAR.

4: FOCUS ON THE COLORING DETAIL. HOW IT LOOKS, HOW IT FEELS TO YOU.

5: STRENGTHEN MIND SIGNALS BY CHOOSING COLORS THAT MAKE YOU FEEL GOOD. PICTURE THESE FEELINGS WHILE USING THOSE COLORS.

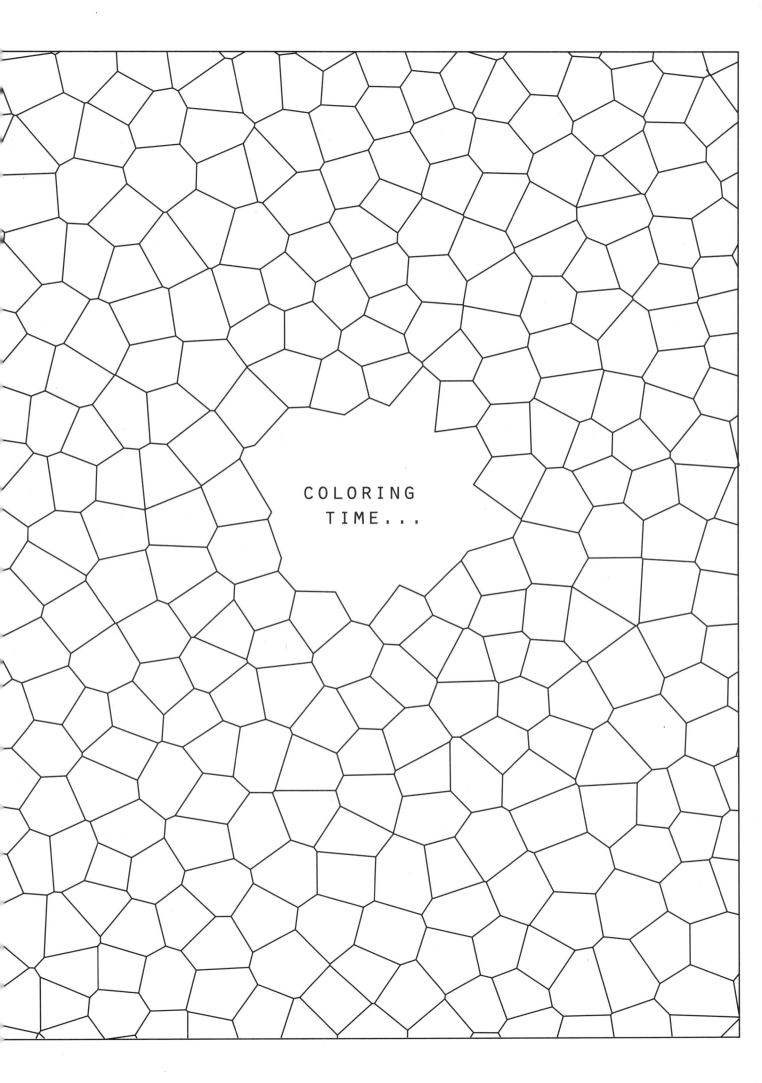

COLORING
TIME...

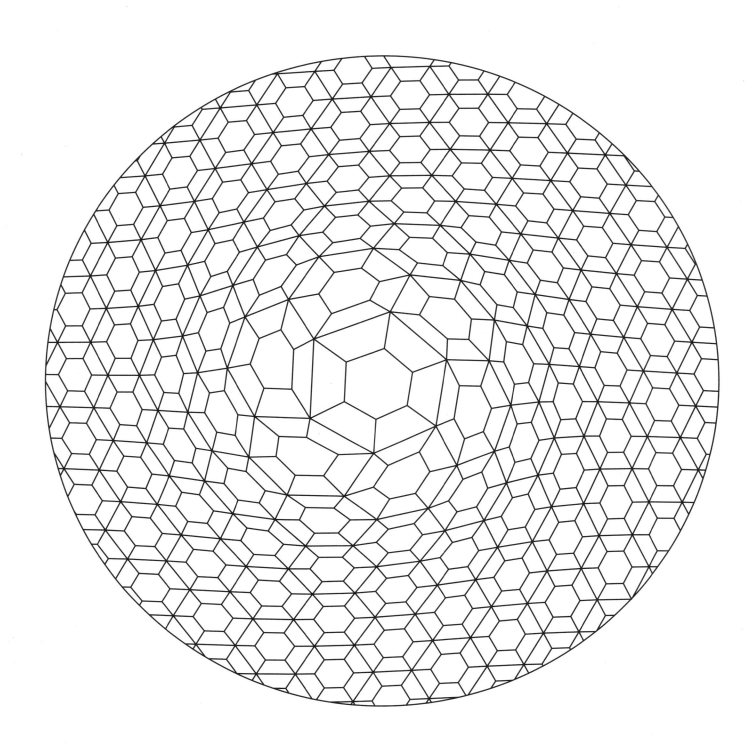

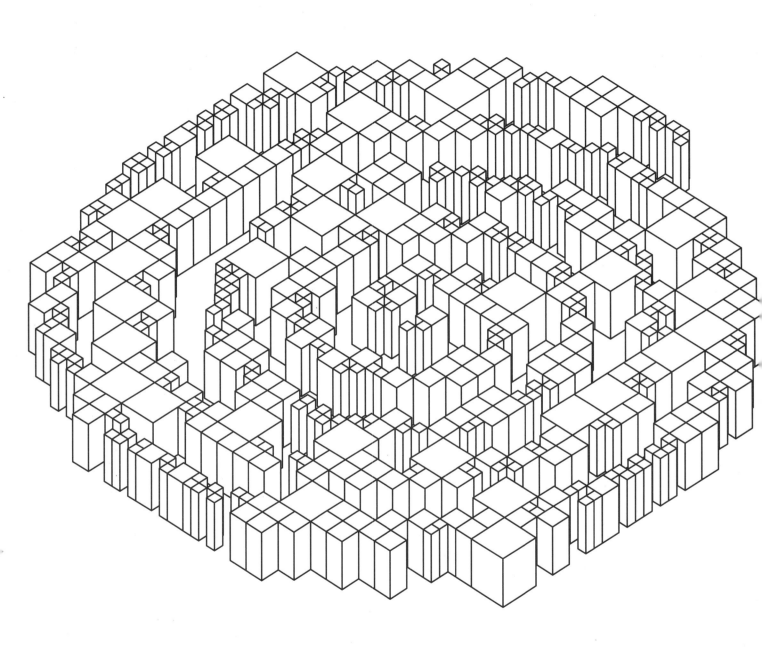

Published in 2016 by Hardie Grant Books

Hardie Grant Books (Australia)
Ground Floor, Building 1
658 Church Street
Richmond, Victoria 3121
www.hardiegrant.com.au

Hardie Grant Books (UK)
5th & 6th Floors
52–54 Southwark Street
London SE1 1UN
www.hardiegrant.co.uk

A Cataloguing-in-Publication entry is available from the catalogue of
the National Library of Australia at www.nla.gov.au
Brain-science: Coloring for agility and fast learning
ISBN 9781743791882

Website: www.colourtation.com
Facebook: www.facebook.com/colourtation
Instagram: @colourtation

Cover, illustrations and text design by Jack Dowling
Printed in Canada by Friesens